CW01149892

Original title:
Hiccups and Daydreams

Copyright © 2024 Creative Arts Management OÜ
All rights reserved.

Author: Giselle Montgomery
ISBN HARDBACK: 978-9916-90-354-4
ISBN PAPERBACK: 978-9916-90-355-1

Echoes of a Wandering Mind

Whispers in the night sky,
Thoughts drift like distant stars,
Chasing shadows of the past,
Lost in the echoes of time.

Fragments of what once was,
Carried on the winds of fate,
Memory's gentle touch,
Fading as the dawn arrives.

Sudden Interruptions of Thought

A moment caught in silence,
Thoughts collide like thunder,
Racing against the clock,
Time slips through my fingers.

A spark ignites the stillness,
Brighter than the morning light,
Ideas swirl and dance,
Lost in the chaos of now.

Lullabies of the Unseen

Soft whispers in the dark,
Songs of dreams yet to bloom,
Unseen hands weave tales,
Gentle like a fading sigh.

Crickets serenade the night,
The moon guides the weary heart,
Wrapped in the night's embrace,
Resting in shadows of peace.

Staccato Dreams

Fragmented visions flash,
A heartbeat in disarray,
Bursting like fleeting stars,
Dancing in a restless haze.

Rhythms clash and collide,
Syncopated thoughts emerge,
Brief moments of clarity,
Lost in the swell of night.

The Jolt of Imagination

In the quiet of night,
Stars start to weave tales,
Colors dance in the sky,
Whispers of dreams prevail.

Thoughts spark like lightning,
A canvas waits for hues,
Where visions come alive,
And fantasies break through.

Time bends in this space,
Ideas take their flight,
With every stroke and shade,
We paint our own light.

Illusions wrapped in gold,
A treasure to behold,
In the mirth of creation,
Our spirits unfold.

Chasing Illusions

Across the sandy dunes,
Footprints fade with the tide,
Chasing shadows of hope,
Where dreams and fears collide.

Mirages gleam ahead,
A sparkle, then they fade,
With every step we take,
New paths are often laid.

In the mirror of time,
Reflections twist and turn,
We seek what is not there,
Yet still, our hearts yearn.

Through the mist of the day,
We wander, lost but free,
In the chase of our thoughts,
We find our destiny.

Flickers of Reverie

A candle's gentle glow,
Illuminates the dark,
Flickers in the silence,
Igniting the small spark.

Thoughts drift like soft clouds,
In the evening's embrace,
Each moment a treasure,
In this tranquil space.

We weave our dreams in night,
A tapestry of sound,
With whispers of the past,
Where lost souls are found.

In the stillness of time,
Fragments of joy unite,
As flickers of reverie,
Guide us into the light.

Moments Between Breaths

In the hush of the dawn,
A heartbeat can be heard,
Between promises made,
And every gentle word.

Time pauses in silence,
As whispers fill the air,
Moments pure and fleeting,
A dance beyond compare.

In the blink of an eye,
Life's essence slips away,
But in those small seconds,
The soul learns how to play.

So hold tight to each breath,
Let the world fade away,
For in those quiet moments,
True magic comes to stay.

Whispers of Starlit Echoes

In the hush of night's embrace,
Stars weave tales of timeless grace.
Moonlight dances on the streams,
Echoes whisper, lost in dreams.

Softly glows the silver light,
Guiding hearts through softest flight.
Each glimmer holds a secret deep,
In the shadows, memories sleep.

Flutters of the Mind's Wander

Thoughts like butterflies take flight,
Chasing colors, pure delight.
Through the meadow, wild and free,
Mind's enchantment, let it be.

With each flutter, whispers sigh,
Echoes of the days gone by.
In the quiet, freedom sings,
Capturing the joy it brings.

Serenade of Sudden Spins

Twirl amidst the dizzy glow,
Life unfolds in sudden flow.
Moments intertwine and blend,
As the world begins to bend.

Laughter swirls in playful arcs,
Lighting up the evening parks.
With each spin, a heartbeat found,
In the joy that swirls around.

Chasing Fancies in the Midst

In the maze where dreams take flight,
Chasing fancies through the night.
Each desire a fleeting ghost,
In the shadows, we shall coast.

Through the mist, we seek a chance,
Glimmers spark a daring dance.
In this realm where hopes entwine,
Chasing fancies, yours and mine.

Unruly Muses

In shadows they whisper, elusive and loud,
Dancing on edges of laughter and doubt.
They tug at the heart, demand to be freed,
With wild abandon, they sow every seed.

They flutter like leaves in a restless breeze,
Twisting and turning, they tease and they please.
From chaos they weave, a tapestry bright,
An unruly canvas, where dreams take their flight.

Echoes of brilliance in moments unchained,
Glimpses of truth in the madness unframed.
With each fleeting spark, they ignite and they fade,
These muses that tantalize, never afraid.

Yet still we pursue them, these spirits so bold,
In the silence of night, their stories unfold.
Unruly and tempestuous, soft as a sigh,
They linger in whispers, while we learn to fly.

Glimpses Beyond the Veil

In twilight's embrace, secrets unfold,
Silent connections, a glimpse into gold.
The veil that divides, so thin and so frail,
Hints at the stories that dwell beyond pale.

Mysteries whisper through shadows of dusk,
Phantoms of past in a world rich with musk.
We strain to perceive what our eyes cannot see,
In the flicker of stars, they beckon to be.

Lost in the echoes of heartbeats entwined,
The sacred and mundane, forever aligned.
With faith as our lantern, we step through the night,
Seeking the truths that hide just from sight.

In silence we gather, as destinies thread,
For glimpses beyond the veil gently spread.
Each moment a whisper, a touch like a sigh,
Connecting the realms where our spirits can fly.

Mirage of the Mind

Thoughts drift like phantoms in vast open air,
Shifting and swirling, a dance rare and rare.
A mirage of wisdom, it teases the eye,
Unraveling visions that flicker and fly.

What's real and what's not in this labyrinth maze?
Each turn leads to echoes of shimmering days.
Illusions of clarity, fragments ignite,
The mind plays a game, blurring day into night.

Memories shimmer like stars in the dark,
Fleeting like fireflies, they leave but a spark.
In whispers they linger, elusive yet clear,
A canvas of thoughts, both precious and dear.

Each moment we grasp slides away like the sand,
Leaving us stranded, unsure of the land.
Yet in the confusion, there's beauty to find,
A mirage of hope lies within the mind.

Glimpses Beyond the Veil

In twilight's embrace, secrets unfold,
Silent connections, a glimpse into gold.
The veil that divides, so thin and so frail,
Hints at the stories that dwell beyond pale.

Mysteries whisper through shadows of dusk,
Phantoms of past in a world rich with musk.
We strain to perceive what our eyes cannot see,
In the flicker of stars, they beckon to be.

Lost in the echoes of heartbeats entwined,
The sacred and mundane, forever aligned.
With faith as our lantern, we step through the night,
Seeking the truths that hide just from sight.

In silence we gather, as destinies thread,
For glimpses beyond the veil gently spread.
Each moment a whisper, a touch like a sigh,
Connecting the realms where our spirits can fly.

Mirage of the Mind

Thoughts drift like phantoms in vast open air,
Shifting and swirling, a dance rare and rare.
A mirage of wisdom, it teases the eye,
Unraveling visions that flicker and fly.

What's real and what's not in this labyrinth maze?
Each turn leads to echoes of shimmering days.
Illusions of clarity, fragments ignite,
The mind plays a game, blurring day into night.

Memories shimmer like stars in the dark,
Fleeting like fireflies, they leave but a spark.
In whispers they linger, elusive yet clear,
A canvas of thoughts, both precious and dear.

Each moment we grasp slides away like the sand,
Leaving us stranded, unsure of the land.
Yet in the confusion, there's beauty to find,
A mirage of hope lies within the mind.

Stutters in Serenity

Moments of stillness, wrapped up in a sigh,
Echoes of silence beneath the wide sky.
In tranquil reflections, the heart starts to race,
Stutters in serenity, time finds its place.

Gentle the rhythm of breath on the breeze,
Fluttering softly like whispers through trees.
A heartbeat forgotten, a pause in the song,
Melodies linger, where we all feel belong.

Yet anxiety dances, a shadow so close,
In stillness it flickers, a delicate ghost.
Each second a heartbeat, a fleeting embrace,
Stutters in serenity, a soft, fleeting grace.

In the balance we find the peace and the strife,
Moments that tether the pulse of our life.
Through chaos and calm, we navigate the tide,
Finding our footing where stutters reside.

Tangles of the Mind

Thoughts weave and twist like vines,
In shadows where silence binds.
A labyrinth of hopes and fears,
Echoes fading through the years.

Threads of doubt pull at my core,
Whispers lost behind closed doors.
Clarity, a distant gleam,
Drifting far from what I dream.

Moments flicker, lost in haze,
Cascading thoughts in endless maze.
Finding peace in chaos near,
Navigating through the fear.

Yet within these tangled lines,
A spark of joy gently shines.
In the chaos, I will find,
The beauty of a tangled mind.

Quirks of the Soul

Dancing shadows play and twist,
In the silence, thoughts persist.
Whimsical paths that winds unfold,
Stories written, yet untold.

Curious heart with vivid dreams,
Flowing gently like mountain streams.
In the laughter, quirks reside,
Whispers of the soul's bright tide.

Colors fading, then anew,
Fragments of a vibrant hue.
Every twist, each turn defined,
In the corners of the mind.

Embrace the odd, the strange, the free,
Unraveling the mystery.
For within the quirks we find,
A tapestry of the soul entwined.

Seasons of Disturbance

Winter's chill grips tight the night,
Fallen leaves spread ghostly white.
Storms of change rage wild and free,
Whispering truths we seldom see.

Spring awakens with a sigh,
Fractured dreams beneath the sky.
Buds of hope push through the ground,
In the chaos, peace is found.

Summer burns with fiery light,
Sparks of passion, bold and bright.
Yet the shadows linger long,
Echoes of a silent song.

Autumn's breath brings soft decay,
In its beauty, hearts may sway.
As each season shifts in turn,
Lessons of disturbance, learn.

Fleeting Fantasies

Chasing dreams on whispered winds,
Elusive threads that break and bend.
In the twilight, visions gleam,
Fleeting moments lost in dream.

Laughter dances in the air,
Magic moments, scarce and rare.
A fleeting glimpse of joy so bright,
Evanescent as the night.

Shadows cast by fading light,
Hope flickers, just out of sight.
In the chase, we find our way,
Through the night into the day.

Hold the cherished, let them flow,
In the heart where dreams may grow.
For every fantasy that fades,
Leaves behind sweet serenades.

Twists of Serendipity

In the dance of chance, we find,
Paths unwritten, sweetly intertwined.
Moments whisper, secrets unfold,
Stories born from hearts so bold.

Fate's gentle nudge, a guiding light,
Leading us to love's pure delight.
Unexpected joys, a joyful spark,
In the darkest corners, hope leaves a mark.

Traces of a Stammered Heart

Words falter, a hesitant start,
Emotions crashing, a timid heart.
Each beat echoes, a silent plea,
Longing for the voice to be free.

In shadows deep, true feelings hide,
Yearning for courage, they bide their time.
As light breaks in, the silence fades,
The stammered heart seeks love's cascade.

Daylight Disruptions

Morning breaks, a new day born,
Yet shadows linger, dreams are torn.
Sunlight chases the dark away,
Yet echoes of night still softly sway.

Winds of change, a fierce embrace,
Time weaves patterns we can't erase.
In daylight's glow, truths collide,
Unraveling secrets that darkness can't hide.

Echoes of the Mind's Eye

Thoughts like waves crash on the shore,
Whispers of memories, evermore.
In the quietude, visions arise,
Reflections dance behind closed eyes.

Fragments of dreams, entwined with fear,
Stories of laughter, shed a tear.
In the gallery of the mind's embrace,
We find the shadows of time and space.

Interludes Between Moments of Delight

In quiet corners, whispers draw,
Fleeting smiles caught in the light.
Time bends softly as we pause,
Savoring dreams that take flight.

A sunbeam dances on the floor,
Echoing laughter, pure and bright.
Memories linger, asking for more,
Holding close the warmth of night.

Each heartbeat, a tender refrain,
Sips of joy in twilight's embrace.
With every sigh, we find our gain,
In sweetness found in time's grace.

As stars emerge and fade away,
We cherish these moments, so rare.
Interludes of the heart's ballet,
A tapestry woven with care.

The Jitter of Inspiration's Dance

Fingers tap against the page,
A melody springs to life.
Thoughts collide, a vibrant stage,
Where whispers banish all strife.

Colors clash and words entwine,
Electric sparks in vibrant hue.
Crafting realms where dreams align,
The jittering muse sees us through.

In every turn, a chance afforded,
To leap beyond the known refrain.
From silent flows, ideas lauded,
Inspiration dances, unchained.

We dive into the swirling sea,
Where every stroke paints our truth.
Letting go, we set it free,
Embracing the joy of our youth.

Lulls of Wonder in Midair

Suspended moments grace the sky,
A soft hush in the afternoon.
Clouds drift lazily, passing by,
While time harmonizes with tune.

Among the branches, shadows play,
Dance of light, in whispers, light.
Nature's lullabies softly sway,
Cradling hearts in pure delight.

Each breeze carries a tale unwound,
Of dreams that twirl in carefree flight.
In the vastness, magic is found,
Lulls of wonder, our true respite.

We bask in peace like gentle streams,
Flowing onward, ever so clear.
In these lulls, we weave our dreams,
Finding solace, holding them near.

Jumps of Heart amid Floating Hues

Above the world, we leap with grace,
Colors whirl in vibrant fire.
With every bound, we find our place,
A canvas born from pure desire.

Balloons of laughter fill the air,
As hearts collide in joyous flight.
Each moment savored, free from care,
In the dance of day and night.

In twilight's glow, we take our chance,
With every jump, we touch the sky.
Floating hues entice our dance,
In these colors, we learn to fly.

Together, we embrace the thrill,
Amidst the dreams in which we play.
With jumps of heart, our spirits fill,
A joyous echo, come what may.

Interruptions of Infinity

Whispers of time drift and sway,
Eternal echoes lead us astray.
Moments collide like stars in the night,
Each fragment a spark, a fleeting light.

Endless cycles of laughter and tears,
Carving our paths through hope and fears.
Infinity hums its elusive song,
In every silence, we all belong.

Threads of existence weave and unwind,
The fabric of fate, intricately kind.
Interruptions define our grand quest,
In chaos, we find a moment of rest.

Through the corridors of what might be,
We chase shadows of our memory.
In the dance of the infinite space,
We grasp at the void; we embrace the grace.

Unraveled Thoughts

In the quiet corners of the mind,
Thoughts unravel, seeking to remind.
Like threads of silk in a tangled skein,
Each idea whispers, joy, or pain.

Fragments float, scattered like leaves,
In the autumn of dreams, the heart believes.
Moments of clarity, fleeting and slight,
Illuminate shadows, bring forth the light.

Questions bloom like petals in spring,
Curiosity pulls at the heartstring.
Unraveled ideas, a woven tapestry,
Constructing meaning from the mystery.

Stories lie dormant, waiting to rise,
To dance in the rain or beneath the skies.
Each thought a drop in the ocean vast,
Together they echo, future and past.

Fractured Fairy Tales

Once upon a time, the story broke,
Heroes and villains, dreams awoke.
Charmed by the whims of fate's hand,
In fractured realms, they try to stand.

Whispers of magic fill the air,
Yet darkness lingers, unaware.
Curses weave through the nights so deep,
In shattered mirrors, secrets keep.

Love's embrace wrapped in thorns, so tight,
The heart's desire dances with fright.
Once gleaming crowns now dust and rust,
In the tales of hope, we place our trust.

Amidst the ruins of once fairy land,
New stories form; together we stand.
For in every fracture, a lesson lays,
In the heart of darkness, the light still plays.

The Chaos of Quietude

In silence lies a tempest's roar,
Hidden turmoil behind closed door.
Whispers of thoughts swirl in the void,
Where dreams collide and peace is toyed.

Moments stretch like shadows at dawn,
In stillness, the heart feels withdrawn.
Chaos dances softly in the air,
Yet tranquility lingers, a muted prayer.

The mind's labyrinth, a curious maze,
In quietude's grip, we drift and gaze.
Finding solace in the noise within,
A paradox of peace and fervor spins.

Through quiet chaos, we search for light,
Navigating shadows within the night.
In still waters, deep truths reside,
Embracing the chaos, we learn to glide.

Echoes of the Heart's Leap

In the stillness of the night,
Whispers flutter soft and light,
Memories drift like gentle streams,
Echoes dancing in our dreams.

Hearts entwined in silent song,
A rhythm beautiful and strong,
Every beat a tale retold,
Woven threads of joy and gold.

Through the valleys, over hills,
The heart's leap gives the spirit thrills,
No distance can our love erase,
In every echo, find your place.

Let the echoes guide the way,
In twilight's fading, we will stay,
Together bound, forever near,
In the echoes, love is clear.

The Pulse of a Wandering Soul

Under skies of endless blue,
A wandering soul seeks what's true,
With every step, the pulse grows strong,
In the rhythm, where I belong.

Mountains high and valleys low,
Every path starts to flow,
Each heartbeat a call to roam,
In the wild, I find my home.

Stars above, they guide the night,
In their glow, I find my light,
Through the dark and endless miles,
A wandering soul finds its smiles.

Embrace the journey, feel the beat,
In every corner, joy and heat,
Life is pulse, a rhythmic dance,
In wandering, I find my chance.

Serendipity in Shadows

In the corners where shadows play,
Serendipity lights the way,
Unexpected joy, a sweet embrace,
In twilight's arms, we find our space.

Laughter echoes, soft and sweet,
Moments stumble on gentle feet,
In fleeting glances, spirits weave,
A dance of fate, we dare believe.

Through the night, discoveries call,
In shadows deep, we rise, we fall,
With open hearts, we face the dawn,
Serendipity leads us on.

Each shadow holds a secret dear,
In whispers soft, they draw us near,
Through faded light, love's truth is known,
In serendipity, we're never alone.

Brief Respite of Delight

In the garden where flowers bloom,
A moment's pause dispels the gloom,
Colors dance in the gentle breeze,
A brief respite, a heart at ease.

Sunlight gleams on dewy grass,
Time slows down as moments pass,
In laughter shared, we find our way,
Delight blooms brighter day by day.

With every petal, joy unfolds,
Simple pleasures, stories told,
In fleeting thoughts, we find our grace,
In brief respites, we embrace.

Let memories linger, soft and bright,
In these moments, hearts take flight,
Life's little joys, pure and slight,
In brief respites, find the light.

Jumps in the Flow

In the river's gentle stream,
Currents pull and drift along,
Every leap a fleeting dream,
Echoes of a vibrant song.

Shapes of shadows dance on light,
Ripples weave a tale so grand,
In the chaos, pure delight,
Flowing softly, hand in hand.

As the moments rise and fall,
Time a friend, a fleeting guest,
Jumps of joy, we heed the call,
Finding peace within the jest.

Let us glide and sway with grace,
In a rhythm that's our own,
Every heartbeat finds its place,
In the flow, we have grown.

A Lull in the Journey

Winding roads beneath the stars,
Whispers soft, the night is still,
In the quiet, peace mars,
Time slows down, a gentle chill.

Clouds drift in a velvet sky,
Each breath deeper, filling space,
Moments pause, we wonder why,
The journey's not a frantic race.

Underneath the silver moon,
Thoughts like leaves begin to fall,
In this lull, there's space for tune,
Listening close, we heed the call.

Dreams take flight, soft sighs ignite,
In the calm, our spirits soar,
Every heartbeat feels so light,
A lull that opens every door.

Thoughts Like Fireflies

In the dusk, they start to shine,
Tiny sparks of fleeting thought,
Each a glimmer, yours and mine,
Magic captured, never caught.

Flickering in tangled night,
They dance on whispers of the breeze,
Chasing shadows, pure delight,
Carving paths through darkened trees.

Similar to our wandering mind,
Searching for the breath of light,
Unruly visions intertwined,
Filling essence with their flight.

So let thoughts like fireflies bloom,
Illuminate the darkened way,
In their glow, dispel the gloom,
Dancing freely, come what may.

The Dance of Spontaneity

In the moment, seize the flame,
Let the music guide our feet,
Every step a playful game,
Rhythms pulse, our hearts in heat.

Twisting, turning, lost in bliss,
No rehearsal, pure delight,
In this chaos, find the kiss,
Of freedom's dance, the world takes flight.

Embrace the wild, let go the plan,
Here and now, we stake our claim,
In every twirl, discover span,
Where spontaneity's not the same.

Join the whirlwind, let it flow,
In the heart of night we sway,
With every leap, the spirit grow,
Together in the dance, we stay.

Fabled Distractions

In shadows dance the ancient tales,
Whispers lost in moonlit gales.
Fables weave through time's embrace,
Chasing dreams in a wistful space.

Sirens sing from distant shores,
Tempting hearts with open doors.
Each glance a spark, a fleeting fire,
Binding souls to dreams desire.

Cloaked in fog, the pathways bend,
Leading wanderers to pretend.
Yet in the mist, a truth does glow,
With every step, new stories flow.

In this realm of sparkling light,
Fabled distractions, pure delight.
With every sigh, a new undone,
Lost in the tale, we become one.

Lingering Whims

Echoes drift like feathered dreams,
In the heart where longing gleams.
A moment caught, a breath in time,
Whims of the soul, a whispered rhyme.

Dancing leaves in autumn's grace,
Each turn a step, a new embrace.
Fleeting thoughts like clouds parade,
In the mind where wishes fade.

Fingers trace the edge of night,
Seeking solace in the light.
Lingering whims, they softly play,
Guiding hearts, come what may.

Amidst the noise, a silence sings,
Of cherished dreams and fragile things.
Embrace the dance of what might be,
In life's vast sea, we are set free.

A Symphony of Breath

Inhale the dawn, the day begins,
A melody where life spins.
Each heartbeat echoes, soft and clear,
A symphony that draws us near.

Rustling leaves in harmony,
Nature's song, wild and free.
The whispering wind, a gentle guide,
In this rhythm, we confide.

With every sigh, a note is played,
In silence where memories stayed.
A dance of breaths, entwined as one,
Underneath the rising sun.

Feel the pulse of life around,
In every breath, a sacred sound.
Together we compose the score,
A symphony forevermore.

Fragments of the Unconscious

In starlit nights, our spirits roam,
Through shadows cast, we find our home.
Fragments whispered, softly found,
Echoes linger all around.

Dreams woven in twilight's thread,
Where thoughts and wishes long to tread.
Fleeting visions spark a flame,
In the quiet, they call our name.

What lies beneath the surface deep?
Secrets tucked where silence sleeps.
In fragments small, the whole reveals,
The truth of what the heart concealed.

Through the haze, we glimpse our path,
In shadows cast by hidden wrath.
Fragments of the mind's embrace,
Awake, we dance in time and space.

The Breach of Solitude

In silence deep, the shadows weave,
A fragile heart, not yet to grieve.
The echo's call, a distant friend,
Where solitude begins to bend.

A flicker light, a whispered name,
In corners dark, a daring flame.
The walls may close, but hope arise,
Through cracks of time, beneath the skies.

The softest sigh, the wildest dream,
Transcends the night, a silver beam.
Each moment caught, a breath, a glance,
In solitude, we find our dance.

When shadows fade, the dawn will break,
With every step, the heart will wake.
In breach of quiet, find your tune,
Embrace the day, the sun, the moon.

Dreams on a Whim

In slumber's grasp, the visions flow,
A fleeting thought, a tale to sew.
From lofty heights to valleys low,
In dreams on a whim, we freely go.

A carousel of whispered fears,
We chase the stars, drown in our tears.
Each fleeting glance, a future bright,
In hazy realms, lost to the night.

A canvas vast, where colors swirl,
Within our minds, the fables twirl.
Every heartbeat sparks anew,
In dreams on a whim, we are true.

As morning breaks, the visions fade,
Yet echoes linger, promises made.
With every dawn, a chance reborn,
To chase our dreams, each new day sworn.

A Tangle of Thoughts

In tangled webs, the musings stay,
A spiral dance, come what may.
Threads intertwine, both light and dark,
In every twist, a hidden spark.

The mind a maze, with doors to find,
A restless heart, a tangled mind.
Each scattered piece, a puzzle's part,
To weave the whole, to mend the heart.

In whispers soft, the echoes play,
As fleeting clouds drift far away.
With every turn, a truth unfolds,
In tangled thoughts, new stories told.

Through silent nights, the questions roam,
In chaos found, we build our home.
In tangled threads, we seek the flow,
To forge our path, to learn, to grow.

The Flicker of a Fable

Once upon a time, tales were spun,
In flickering light, where dreams begun.
A tale of hope, of love's embrace,
In whispered words, we find our place.

Through woods so deep, the shadows glide,
With every step, a heart confides.
A flicker glows, the night reveals,
In every fable, the truth appeals.

A spirit bold, a journey wide,
In every turn, the stars our guide.
Through darkened paths, the love shall shine,
In every moment, fate intertwines.

As stories fade, they live anew,
In every heart, a spark rings true.
The flicker of a fable bright,
In us it glows, our endless light.

Whispers on the Wind

In the twilight, shadows dance,
Softly weaving a fleeting chance.
Echoes of love, lost and found,
In the silence, secrets abound.

Carefree whispers twist and swirl,
Carried by breezes, a gentle pearl.
Nature's refrain, both sweet and clear,
Calls to the heart, drawing us near.

Glimmers of hope in dusk's embrace,
Memories linger in this sacred space.
A lullaby sung with every sigh,
As stars awaken and dreams fly high.

With each breath, the spirit lifts,
In the hush of night, the heart gifts.
Whispers of dreams, a soft caress,
In the wind, we find our rest.

Wandering Threads of Imagination

Threads of thought in colors bright,
Weaving tales in the depth of night.
Every glance, a story spun,
Together we dream, two hearts as one.

With each moment, visions bloom,
A tapestry rich, dispelling gloom.
Wandering paths, we bravely tread,
Through open skies and dreams widespread.

A canvas vast, where dreams take flight,
Fantastic journeys in the pale moonlight.
We chase the shadows, dance with fire,
In every heartbeat, a whispered desire.

Embracing chaos, exploring the mind,
In tangled webs, true fate we find.
With thread and needle, love we sew,
In the realm of dreams, we freely go.

The Breath of a Dream

In the stillness, a dream takes wing,
Softly it dances, a secret spring.
Whispers of hope blend with the night,
Illuminated stars, radiant light.

Like fragile petals on a breeze,
Each thought a sigh among the trees.
Captured moments in twilight's glow,
The heart's sweet cadence, gentle flow.

In the hush, a promise made,
Dreams awaken, never to fade.
With every heartbeat, we feel the fire,
The breath of a dream, our true desire.

Let us wander through fields of gold,
Where stories of love are silently told.
In the breath of a dream, we'll remain,
An endless journey in blissful refrain.

Scribbles of the Psyche

Lines that curve in chaotic grace,
Sketching emotions we dare not trace.
Thoughts dance wildly, a scribbled thread,
In the labyrinth of the mind, we tread.

Colors clash in vibrant hues,
Memories linger, ancient clues.
Each stroke whispers a hidden tale,
In the quiet, where dreams set sail.

While shadows lengthen, truths unfold,
In frantic scribbles, our hearts are bold.
Thoughts spill like ink, a tempest's call,
In the chaos, we rise and fall.

Embrace the mess, the art divine,
For in the chaos, our souls align.
In scribbles of the psyche, we find release,
A canvas of thoughts, a fleeting peace.

The Unruly Laughter of Lost Thoughts

In shadowed corners of my mind,
The echoes of dreams long left behind.
They chatter and dance in a vibrant spree,
A symphony of chaos, wild and free.

Each fleeting notion, a spark in the night,
Flickers before fading from sight.
They bubble and brew with a giggling cheer,
These unruly whispers that linger near.

Laughter bubbles and fills the air,
Like fragile bubbles, they float with flair.
In the garden of thought, they weave and roll,
A tapestry of noise that stirs the soul.

Though lost from grasp, they will not cease,
These thoughts, they frolic, they grant no peace.
Yet, in their ruckus, a joy I find,
The beauty lies in the playful mind.

Tumbling Toward the Unexpected

Down the hill, I begin to fall,
A twist of fate, a sudden call.
The world blurs past me, colors collide,
I tumble forward, nowhere to hide.

With every twist, a new surprise,
A glimpse of wonder through clouded skies.
The unexpected whispers in my ear,
Guiding me onward, laughter near.

I roll through valleys, I leap through streams,
Chasing the shadows of my dreams.
The path unfolds in a wild dance,
Each stumble and roll feels like a chance.

Tumbling onward, I lose my way,
Yet somehow I find joy in the play.
Unexpected journeys come alive,
In every fall, my heart will thrive.

Trails of Imagination's Journey

On winding paths where dreams unfold,
Imagination breathes, a tale retold.
With each step forward, the world transforms,
Into vibrant realms, where magic warms.

Through forests deep and skies so wide,
I wander freely, with thoughts as my guide.
The stars are maps, the clouds, my muse,
In this boundless place, I cannot lose.

Chasing echoes of stories yet spun,
I trace the lines where fantasies run.
Each thought a flower, each dream a song,
In this wild journey, I feel I belong.

Imagination's trails lead to unknown,
An endless vista where seeds are sown.
With every heartbeat, I come alive,
In the tapestry woven, I forever thrive.

Whispers of Unrest

In the quiet corners of the night,
Whispers stir, a soft, distant fright.
Voices flutter like leaves in a breeze,
Carrying stories lost in the trees.

Restless dreams weave a tangled thread,
Unsettled thoughts, like shadows, spread.
Questions linger, they cling to the air,
In the silence, a weight we share.

Winds of change howl and seize the heart,
Protests of thought, an unlikely art.
A chorus of fears, a melody stark,
In the stillness, ignites a spark.

Though unrest whispers, it also ignites,
The courage to dream and to reach new heights.
In every murmur, a chance to explore,
Whispers of unrest lead to so much more.

Unruly Echoes

In the forest where whispers play,
Voices linger, dancing astray.
A cacophony of dreams takes flight,
Shadows weave through the fading light.

Crimson leaves swirl in the breeze,
Stories entwined with ancient trees.
Each echo a tale, lost yet found,
In this vibrant, enchanted ground.

Songs of the night awaken the stars,
Guided by the moon from afar.
Secrets whispered in twilight's glow,
Unruly echoes, forever flow.

Let not the silence claim its prize,
For within the noise, the heart can rise.
In every echo, a promise stays,
Life's unruly symphony plays.

Dream-Spun Interludes

In the tapestry of night, we weave,
Drifting on shadows, we believe.
Colors of starlight softly blend,
A journey taken with each breath penned.

Moments captured in fleeting dreams,
Within the silence, inspiration gleams.
Time flows gently, like a sweet song,
In the heart's embrace, we belong.

Fragile wishes drift through the air,
A whisper of hope, gentle and fair.
Each interlude unveiled with grace,
In the realm of dreams, we find our place.

Together we dance on the edge of light,
Chasing the dawn, embracing the night.
With every heartbeat, a story spins,
In this realm where our laughter begins.

Awakened Longings

Beneath the bloom of the crescent moon,
Awakened hearts pulse to a tune.
With each breath, a wish takes flight,
Longing for love in the stillness of night.

Silent promises whisper on the breeze,
Entwined souls wander with ease.
In every glance, a spark ignites,
Illuminating pathways, guiding insights.

Tender whispers brush against the skin,
Awakened desires whisper within.
Each moment a promise, an unspoken vow,
In the quiet embrace of the here and now.

Though distance stretches, hearts remain near,
Awakened longings whisper sincere.
In the depth of night, love finds its way,
Through the shadows, it breathes and sways.

Evenings of the Unseen

In the twilight where day meets night,
Unseen magic begins to ignite.
The world holds its breath, pausing in time,
Gentle whispers in rhythm and rhyme.

Softly, the colors of dusk unfurl,
A hidden dance, a fleeting twirl.
In the stillness, secrets take flight,
Evenings of wonder, draped in light.

The stars emerge with tales to tell,
In the silence, enchantments dwell.
Mysteries woven through shadows cast,
Evenings of the unseen, vast.

Let go of worry, embrace the night,
For in darkness, we find our sight.
In the heart of dusk, horizons gleam,
Awaken to life, live the dream.

Gentle Jabs of Unruly Imagination

In twilight's glow, dreams softly tease,
Where thoughts take flight on a playful breeze.
Colors clash in a swirling dance,
Each whisper nudges the mind's romance.

Stars giggle softly, casting their spells,
Bringing forth tales that the heart compels.
Imagination roams, wild and free,
Chasing shadows, just you and me.

Wonders awaken in the quiet night,
As we dare to dream beyond the light.
Gentle jabs push the limits we know,
In this realm, our spirits can grow.

With a wink and a nod, the world rearranges,
In the tapestry of thought, nothing changes.
Each spark ignites a luminous glow,
In the gallery of dreams, let us go.

Breach of Breath in Wandering Minds

Whispers of wind touch the wandering heart,
Breaching the silence, a tender start.
Thoughts drift softly like clouds in the sky,
In the quiet moments, we learn to fly.

A breath unspools the threads of the day,
Wandering minds find their own way.
Each sigh carries a tale of surprise,
In the depths of stillness, the spirit flies.

Through meadows of thought, we gently stroll,
Finding solace in echoes that make us whole.
Breezes invite us to dance and expand,
In the play of the mind, we take a stand.

Every fleeting breath reveals the divine,
In search of the truths that make us align.
Wandering deeper, the treasures we find,
Breach of breath, intertwining the mind.

Puddles of Wonder and Surprise

Raindrops gather in playful pools,
Reflecting the sky, like shimmering jewels.
Children leap in, splashing around,
In each little puddle, new joys abound.

Mirrors of life, capturing light,
Sparks of wonder in each watery sight.
Footprints dissolve, yet laughter remains,
In puddles of magic, we dance in the rains.

Each ripple tells tales of what has been,
In moments of joy, our hearts intervene.
Nature's canvas, a watercolor art,
Puddles connect us, a bridge to the heart.

So let us wander where wonders collide,
In each little puddle, let dreams be our guide.
For in every splash, a story unwinds,
Puddles of wonder awaken our minds.

The Ebb and Flow of Fantastical Whispers

In the hush of night, whispers arise,
Carried on currents that softly mesmerize.
Tales from the sea, where dreams gently crest,
The ebb and flow brings our hearts to rest.

Mysteries linger on the breath of the tide,
In fantastical realms, we take a ride.
Each whisper a promise, a playful tease,
In waves of enchantment, our spirits find ease.

Stars collide in a cosmic ballet,
Guiding our thoughts like boats on the bay.
The whispers of magic, the rhythms we know,
In the dance of the universe, we learn to flow.

As dawn draws near, the whispers subside,
But the echoes within continue to guide.
The ebb of the night, the flow of the day,
In fantastical whispers, we find our way.

Bubbles in Time

Floating gently through the air,
A fragile moment, light as air.
Each bubble tells a fleeting tale,
Of laughter, dreams, and joys that sail.

In sunlight's grasp, they shimmer bright,
Reflecting love, a pure delight.
They rise and pop like whispered sighs,
In fleeting forms, our past complies.

Time rolls on as bubbles burst,
Each memory quenches our thirst.
We chase the echoes, dance with fate,
In every bubble, life creates.

But like the sparrow's fleeting song,
The bubbles drift, but not for long.
They leave a trace, a fond embrace,
In time's expanse, we find our place.

Curious Interruptions

A knock at dawn, a whispered sound,
An unexpected twist astound.
Life ebbs and flows with gentle care,
A fleeting moment, bold and rare.

A child's laughter fills the air,
A stray cat purrs, without a care.
The clock ticks on, yet time stands still,
Curious souls feed wonder's thrill.

In crowded rooms, a gaze will cross,
A glimpse of fate, no path at loss.
Conversations shift with subtle grace,
Interruptions spark a new embrace.

Each moment bends, a soft surprise,
Life's rhythm dances, never dies.
In curious threads, the heart will weave,
Connections made, we dare believe.

Cascades of Surrealism

In dreamlike hues, the landscape sways,
The mind unfurls in twisted ways.
Time drips slowly, colors merge,
In brilliant streams, our thoughts converge.

Fish swim in trees, clouds take flight,
With whispers soft, they ignite the night.
A door leads to the starry seas,
Where visions bloom like whispered trees.

Mirrors fracture, worlds collide,
Reality's veil begins to slide.
We dance on edges, lose our ground,
In cascades wild, our truth is found.

Fragments spark with vivid glee,
Surreal moments set us free.
Through every curve, our spirits glide,
In imaginative trains, we ride.

The Uneven Pulse of Creativity

A heartbeat skips, a thought awakes,
In every stroke, a chance it takes.
Ideas flow like tides at night,
Restless whispers, pure delight.

Sometimes a roar, sometimes a sigh,
A fragile spark, a grouchy cry.
Uneven paths where muses tread,
In chaos born, our dreams are fed.

Colors clash, shapes twist and spin,
With every failure, lessons win.
Creation thrives on jagged lines,
In imperfect forms, true beauty shines.

So let the pulse lead where it may,
Embrace the wild, the bold, the sway.
In creativity's dance, we find our song,
In all its forms, we truly belong.

Bubbles of Thought and Time

In the stillness, ideas bloom,
Floating softly, they drift and zoom.
Captured moments, fleeting sighs,
Bubbles of thought, rise to the skies.

Fleeting whispers, secrets shared,
In the silence, dreams are dared.
Time stretches, bends, and sways,
Bubbles of thought dance in plays.

Colors swirl in electric gleam,
Catch the laughter, catch the dream.
Each bubble carries a gentle spark,
Illuminating the deepest dark.

Time moves softly, like a stream,
Bubbles shimmer in twilight's beam.
They pop with laughter, spark with grace,
In the end, we find our place.

The Quirks of Breath and Reverie

In every breath, a story lies,
Whispers of dreams, beneath the skies.
Quirks of the heart, rhythms entwine,
Dancing in echoes, sweet and divine.

Breath like petals, soft and light,
Catching the stars that shine at night.
Reveries linger, precious and bold,
In the quiet, our tales unfold.

Through puffs of wind, we wander free,
Each sigh a note in our symphony.
Quirks and laughter, woven tight,
In the silence, we share our light.

With every heartbeat, we embrace,
The strange beauty of time and space.
Breath brings us closer, hand in hand,
A quirky reverie, a self-made band.

A Symphony of Stutters and Clouds

In the sky, clouds drift and play,
A symphony softens the light of day.
Stutters of thunder, whispers of grace,
Dreams unfold in the open space.

Each droplet falls like a soft refrain,
Echoing stories of joy and pain.
Clouds dance slow on a canvas grand,
Colors explode as they meet the land.

A symphony mingles with the breeze,
Notes of silence, carried with ease.
Stutters of laughter, melancholy sighs,
In the twilight, the harmony flies.

With every storm, painting the night,
A symphony echoes, pure and bright.
Clouds gather close, united in song,
In this cadence, we all belong.

Pause in the Rhythm of Whimsy

In the dance of leaves, a pause we find,
Whimsy whispers, gentle and kind.
Moments linger like sunlight's glow,
Dancing softly, to and fro.

With every laugh, a step is traced,
In this rhythm, time is chased.
Whimsy flows like a river's song,
In the stillness, we all belong.

Take a breath, let moments sway,
Pause in the magic of the day.
Each second holds a universe vast,
In the rhythm of life, we are cast.

So let us wander, hand in hand,
Through the whispers of an unseen land.
In the pause, we find our chance,
To live and love in this dance.

The Pause of a Thousand Wishes

In twilight's glow, dreams softly sigh,
A million hopes beneath the sky.
Whispers linger in the fading light,
As stars awaken, shimmering bright.

Hearts hold secrets sealed in gold,
Stories of ages quietly told.
Each wish a flicker, a fleeting flame,
In the stillness, none are the same.

Time stands still, a breath we share,
Echoes of longing blend with air.
With every heartbeat, wishes tread,
In silence, where all paths are spread.

The pause of dreams is rich and deep,
A tapestry of hope we keep.
In shadows cast by the waxing moon,
Our wishes dance, a softened tune.

Breaths in the Breeze

Gentle whispers through swaying trees,
Nature's breath carried by the breeze.
Softly weaving through fields of dreams,
Each sigh a story, softly gleams.

Petals flutter like thoughts that race,
In every moment, find your place.
The world awakens with every hum,
A chorus of life, a vibrant drum.

In laughter shared beneath the sun,
Hearts beat freely, a dance begun.
With every gust, we gamble and sway,
Breaths in the breeze sweep troubles away.

A tranquil pause where spirits fly,
Under the vast, embracing sky.
Let's chase the whispers, feel them near,
For in this moment, we are clear.

The Unexpected Pause

Amidst the rush, a stillness found,
A moment's grace, where dreams abound.
Surprise encircles like a loving embrace,
Time pauses softly in this sacred space.

Thoughts collide and then retreat,
In the hush, our hearts find beat.
The world spins slow, a fleeting glance,
Caught in wonder, we take a chance.

With every breath, the silence grows,
A canvas for thoughts that gently flows.
In quietude, possibilities expand,
In unexpected ways, we understand.

The pause reveals what we forget,
The beauty wrapped in calm and yet.
From chaos, order starts to bloom,
In the unexpected, life finds room.

Breaths in the Breeze

Gentle whispers through swaying trees,
Nature's breath carried by the breeze.
Softly weaving through fields of dreams,
Each sigh a story, softly gleams.

Petals flutter like thoughts that race,
In every moment, find your place.
The world awakens with every hum,
A chorus of life, a vibrant drum.

In laughter shared beneath the sun,
Hearts beat freely, a dance begun.
With every gust, we gamble and sway,
Breaths in the breeze sweep troubles away.

A tranquil pause where spirits fly,
Under the vast, embracing sky.
Let's chase the whispers, feel them near,
For in this moment, we are clear.

The Unexpected Pause

Amidst the rush, a stillness found,
A moment's grace, where dreams abound.
Surprise encircles like a loving embrace,
Time pauses softly in this sacred space.

Thoughts collide and then retreat,
In the hush, our hearts find beat.
The world spins slow, a fleeting glance,
Caught in wonder, we take a chance.

With every breath, the silence grows,
A canvas for thoughts that gently flows.
In quietude, possibilities expand,
In unexpected ways, we understand.

The pause reveals what we forget,
The beauty wrapped in calm and yet.
From chaos, order starts to bloom,
In the unexpected, life finds room.

Fantasies in Flight

On wings of dreams, our fancies soar,
Through endless skies, we yearn for more.
A canvas vast, where visions play,
In night's embrace, we drift away.

Serenades of stars invite our hearts,
To dance in realms where magic starts.
With gentle whispers, hope alights,
Fantasies woven in starlit nights.

Clouds become tales on which we ride,
Where imaginations never hide.
Through cosmic winds, our spirits glide,
In this ethereal space, confide.

Each thought a creature, wild and free,
In dreams, we wander, endlessly.
With every heartbeat, we take flight,
Embracing fantasies, pure delight.

Tides of Fancy

Waves of dreams crash on the shore,
Whispers of wishes, begging for more.
Ebbing gently, carrying hope,
In the moon's embrace, we learn to cope.

With every rise, new stories unfold,
Secrets of the sea, brave and bold.
Dancing shadows and shimmering light,
In tidal rhythms, our spirits take flight.

Drifting clouds paint the sky's dome,
Each hue a memory, each gust a poem.
As the tide shifts, we find our way,
In this dance of fancy, we choose to stay.

Hold the moment, let it breathe,
In the heart of the waves, our hopes we weave.
For every tide brings a chance anew,
To explore the depths, and to dream true.

Clips of Inspiration

In the stillness of a rainy day,
Thoughts flutter like leaves, drifting away.
Snippets of joy and bursts of light,
Capture fleeting moments, hold them tight.

Pages turn, and stories collide,
In the dance of words, where dreams reside.
A pencil's stroke, a canvas so bare,
Paints the visions that linger in air.

Sparkling stars scatter thoughts like dust,
In midnight musings, we learn to trust.
Each spark ignites creativity's flame,
Clipping the shadows where doubt lays claim.

Lifting the veil, we choose to see,
The beauty that lies in creativity.
With each new page, a journey begins,
Chasing the whispers of where art spins.

Flashes of Ecstasy

In a moment's breath, we touch the divine,
Heartbeats echo, our spirits entwine.
Electric pulses travel through skin,
In the dance of joy, we let love in.

Colors explode in a vibrant glow,
Every heartbeat speaks, every pulse flows.
Ecstatic laughter fills the night air,
In unison, we rise, forgetting our care.

A symphony plays in the depths of our core,
Each note ignites, urging us to explore.
Like shooting stars in a velvet sky,
Chasing the fleeting, we learn to fly.

Moments collide, time stands still,
In flashes of ecstasy, we drink our fill.
Together we soar, hands held tight,
In the whirlwind of passion, we bask in the light.

Whimsical Disruptions

A twist of fate, a serendipitous chance,
Magic unfolds in a curious dance.
In the midst of chaos, laughter ignites,
As whimsy appears in the softest of lights.

Unexpected moments, like autumn leaves,
Swirling and twirling, our spirit believes.
Through cracked sidewalks and painted walls,
We find the beauty where chaos calls.

Imagination reigns in the heart of the wild,
In every disruption, there's joy to be filed.
Embrace the absurd, let spontaneity flow,
In whimsical disruptions, find love's glow.

For life is a canvas, messy and bright,
In every splatter, there's brilliance in sight.
So dance with the chaos, let it unfold,
In this whimsical world, let your heart be bold.

Breaths Caught in Reverie's Snare

In the still of twilight's grace,
Shadows dance, a timeless chase.
Whispers soft like autumn leaves,
Caught in dreams, the heart believes.

A world of thoughts begins to swell,
Echoes of a distant bell.
Fingers trace the edge of night,
Capturing the fading light.

Stars engage in playful jest,
Cradling wishes in their rest.
In this realm where wonders flow,
Breaths entwined with time's soft glow.

Let the moon unveil her song,
Where the lost and found belong.
In reverie's embrace we find,
The secrets whispered, hearts aligned.

The Wisp of a Napping Thought

Gentle dreams begin to rise,
Like the mist beneath the skies.
A thought drifts on a feathered breeze,
Wrapped in slumber's sweet reprise.

Like a cat that purrs in light,
Lazy moments take their flight.
Thoughts meander, finding grace,
In their soft and secret space.

Winking stars in quiet sleep,
Cradles where reflections creep.
A wisp of mind, a dainty thread,
Weaving tales yet to be said.

Amid the hush, in shadows deep,
Curiosity will leap.
On the edges of the night,
Napping thoughts will spark delight.

Ecstatic Interruptions in Musing

Sudden bursts of thought arise,
In the stillness, a surprise.
Moments fight the pull of time,
Jubilant, they twist and climb.

Every pause a chance to leap,
Mind awash in hues so deep.
Ideas swirl like autumn rain,
Dancing free from logic's chain.

In the cracks where silence breathes,
Glimmers of imagination weaves.
Joy erupts from quiet thoughts,
Ecstasy in shadows caught.

Laughter echoes, ideas play,
Fleeting glimpses light the way.
In this chaos, joy takes flight,
Musing blooms in beams of light.

The Sway of Surreal Moments

Time malleable, bends and sways,
In the grace of dreamlike lays.
Every thought a spiral dance,
Adrift in an enchanted trance.

Colors bleed in twilight's hue,
Unraveling what we thought true.
Floating softly through the air,
Moments sway, a tender flare.

Whispers tell of worlds unknown,
In the mind, seeds of chance are sown.
Life's edges blur, the heart explores,
Each surreal path, an open door.

Magic lingers, soft and bold,
In the stories yet untold.
Here we dance, unchained, in flight,
Swaying in the fabric of night.

Variations on Daylight's Pause

In the hush of twilight's glow,
Shadows stretch, a soft tableau,
Colors bleed, they merge and fade,
A moment's peace in light conveyed.

Whispers linger, dusk draws near,
The sun dips low, it disappears,
In every hue, a story weaves,
Nature sighs, the heart believes.

Stars awaken, dance on high,
While the moon begins to sigh,
A promise held in twilight's grace,
Time stands still in this embrace.

Dreams unravel, gently spin,
In this realm, where night begins,
Let your spirit take its flight,
In the magic of the night.

Floating Freely in Lunatic Skies

Wandering amidst the cosmic flow,
Where the wildest visions grow,
Thoughts unfurl like clouds on high,
Painting dreams across the sky.

Galaxies twirl in a sweet ballet,
Carving paths where lost souls stray,
In this dance, we drift away,
Floating free, come what may.

Stardust whispers secrets bold,
Stories of the young and old,
In every glimmer, every spark,
Hope ignites within the dark.

Soar with me through realms untamed,
Each heartbeat joyously named,
Among the stars, let our hearts fly,
Floating freely in lunatic sky.

The Gentle Jolt of Fancy

In the pulse of a vivid dream,
Imagination's golden beam,
A tender nudge, a playful tease,
Where thoughts take wing and drift with ease.

Colors swirl in a dance so bright,
Illuminating the canvas of night,
Each brushstroke, a spark of bliss,
In the realm of the impossible kiss.

Ethereal whispers call my name,
Inviting me to join the game,
With every thought, a story grows,
In this garden where wonder flows.

So let us wander, hand in hand,
In this uncharted, enchanted land,
Where dreams collide in gentle flight,
A jolt of fancy, pure delight.

Flickering Shades of Sweet Escape

In dim-lit corners, shadows play,
Flickering softly, night and day,
Each moment, a ripple in time,
Life unfolds like an ancient rhyme.

Candles flicker, the world slows down,
In their glow, lose the frown,
Let worries drift like autumn leaves,
Embrace the peace that freely weaves.

Here we wander, lost and found,
In gentle hues, we spin around,
Every whisper a soothing song,
In this place where we belong.

So take my hand, let shadows guide,
Into the depths where dreams reside,
In flickering shades, we'll find our grace,
A sweet escape, a warm embrace.

Surges of Whimsy

In the garden where thoughts dance,
Laughter spills like gentle rain.
Colors twirl in a bright romance,
Whispers echo, breaking the mundane.

Dreams float high on painted skies,
Winds carry tales of distant lands.
Imaginations soar, time flies,
Crafting joy with unseen hands.

A flicker here, a giggle there,
Joy unfolds in every glance.
Life delights in the lightest air,
As whimsy leads us in a trance.

And so we chase the fleeting spark,
In a world where fancy roams.
We'll twirl within this vibrant arc,
Forever lost in our own homes.

The Breath Between Worlds

In a twilight space, shadows blend,
Time lingers, soft and slow.
Each heartbeat whispers, 'you transcend',
Two realms meet, a gentle flow.

Ghostly echoes of moments past,
Merge with visions yet to bloom.
In this liminal, stillness casts,
Seeds of futures in the gloom.

Fragrant scents from distant dreams,
Awake within the hush of night.
In silence, wisdom's current gleams,
Illuminating paths of light.

Unseen borders softly fade,
As our souls begin to roam.
In the peace of dusk's cascade,
We find our way, we find our home.

Glances of the Unfathomable

Beneath the stars, our eyes collide,
In depths that words cannot express.
Secrets linger where heartbeats hide,
Mysteries twirl in their caress.

From galaxies to silent seas,
Every glance a universe.
In the quiet, we find the keys,
Unlocking the vast, the diverse.

Time suspends, a fleeting kiss,
Infinite truths in a shared stare.
In the void, we find our bliss,
A connection woven with care.

So we seek in the unknowing,
Tides of fate pull us near.
In glances, the vastness growing,
We touch what is held most dear.

Mosaic of Moments

Each heartbeat a tile in the frame,
Life crafted in colors bright.
Fragments weave stories without a name,
A masterpiece born from sheer light.

We gather minutes, pieces fine,
Memories shaped by laughter and tears.
In shadows cast, our stories intertwine,
An intricate dance through the years.

Soft whispers of time echo near,
Scattered like leaves in autumn's breath.
Each moment, a treasure we hold dear,
A testament of life, not of death.

In this mosaic, we find our way,
United through fragments we share.
The artwork of life in its display,
A beauty beyond compare.

Curiosities of the Day

A whispering breeze brushes by,
Nature's secrets softly sigh.
Each shadow hides a tale untold,
In the light, the world unfolds.

A flicker of wings, a spark of gold,
Moments linger, life unfolds.
A child's laughter fills the air,
Echoes of joy, everywhere.

Morning dew upon the grass,
Glistening gems that come to pass.
Cloud shapes wander, drift and play,
Innocent dreams in bright display.

The sun dips low; day meets night,
Stars emerge, a wondrous sight.
Curiosities cease to dwell,
In twilight's embrace, we find our spell.

Shifts in the Fabric

Threads of time weave through the loom,
Patterns shift, dispelling gloom.
A stitch of memory, a fabric torn,
In each unraveling, new is born.

Seasons change, as shadows fade,
Life's designs, a grand parade.
Whispers in the fibers call,
Echoing stories, one and all.

Each moment stitched with love and care,
Crafting visions, bright and rare.
Beneath the surface, shifts align,
In the tapestry, hearts entwine.

Awake to colors yet unseen,
In the weave of all that's been.
Shifts in the fabric, rich and bold,
Life's mosaic, forever told.

The Yearn for the Unseen

In the depths of a silent night,
Stars whisper secrets, cloaked in light.
Hearts reach out, beyond the veil,
Yearning for journeys where dreams sail.

Soft sighs float on moonlit streams,
Illuminating the darkest dreams.
A spark ignites, a flicker glows,
In the silence, mystery grows.

The unknown calls with a gentle grace,
In every shadow, we find a trace.
Through corridors of time we roam,
Seeking the whispers that lead us home.

The yearn for truths we can't behold,
Lies in stories yet to be told.
With each heartbeat, the world spins new,
In the unseen, our spirits grew.

Shattered Reveries

Fragments fall like broken glass,
Shattered dreams, they slip and pass.
Echoes linger of what once was,
In memories tied without a cause.

Colors bleed in a twilight haze,
Silent screams within the maze.
Voices whisper through the night,
Hopes entwined in fading light.

A picture lost, a fleeting glance,
Lost in the rhythm of life's dance.
But even in ruins, beauty blooms,
In shattered reveries, hope resumes.

From the fragments, a new dawn breaks,
In each heart, the spirit wakes.
Though dreams may shatter, souls will mend,
In the dance of life, we rise again.

Sudden Stirring of the Spirit

A whisper calls from deep within,
Awakening the dormant night,
With every pulse, new dreams begin,
In shadows, flickers dance with light.

The heart ignites, a spark anew,
Unraveling the webs of fear,
As courage blooms in vibrant hue,
The spirit sings, the path is clear.

In silent woods, the mind takes flight,
A journey woven through the stars,
The world unfolds in sheer delight,
With every step that journeys far.

Embrace the stir, the call of fate,
For in the chaos, beauty grows,
A sudden shift, a twist, a break,
The spirit soars as freedom flows.

Jagged Edges of Exploration

In crags and cliffs, the heart does race,
Adventure calls from every height,
Each step reveals its wild embrace,
Where shadows dance to gleam of light.

With trembling hands, we grasp the rope,
A leap of faith, the chasm wide,
In jagged paths, we find our hope,
Through every doubt, the soul shall glide.

The map is blurred, no well-worn trail,
We carve our fate with grit and grace,
Through storms and squalls, we will prevail,
Each jagged edge a new face.

Beyond the cliffs, horizons call,
The unknown whispers secrets bold,
Within the wild, let spirits sprawl,
For we are explorers, free and untold.

Unwritten Paths of Wonder

Upon the dawn, with eyes aglow,
We tread on paths yet unexplored,
With every breath, the magic flows,
A canvas blank, a heartbeat roared.

The whispers of the trees surround,
A melody in every sway,
New stories wait beneath the ground,
Where dreams await the light of day.

With open hearts, we seek the new,
In every turn, a thrill unknown,
The paths unwritten call us through,
To find the seeds that we have sown.

In every corner, wonder peeks,
With gentle hands, we start to write,
The world unfurls, with joy it speaks,
Unwritten paths, our souls ignite.

Jagged Edges of Exploration

In crags and cliffs, the heart does race,
Adventure calls from every height,
Each step reveals its wild embrace,
Where shadows dance to gleam of light.

With trembling hands, we grasp the rope,
A leap of faith, the chasm wide,
In jagged paths, we find our hope,
Through every doubt, the soul shall glide.

The map is blurred, no well-worn trail,
We carve our fate with grit and grace,
Through storms and squalls, we will prevail,
Each jagged edge a new face.

Beyond the cliffs, horizons call,
The unknown whispers secrets bold,
Within the wild, let spirits sprawl,
For we are explorers, free and untold.

Unwritten Paths of Wonder

Upon the dawn, with eyes aglow,
We tread on paths yet unexplored,
With every breath, the magic flows,
A canvas blank, a heartbeat roared.

The whispers of the trees surround,
A melody in every sway,
New stories wait beneath the ground,
Where dreams await the light of day.

With open hearts, we seek the new,
In every turn, a thrill unknown,
The paths unwritten call us through,
To find the seeds that we have sown.

In every corner, wonder peeks,
With gentle hands, we start to write,
The world unfurls, with joy it speaks,
Unwritten paths, our souls ignite.

Chaotic Reflections

In shattered glass, the truth refracts,
A million faces stare in awe,
Each fragment holds its own new facts,
In chaos, find what we once saw.

The mirrors bend and twist our fate,
With voices echoing through the haze,
In turmoil, beauty finds its state,
As light and dark engage in plays.

Every shift creates a spark,
As shadows dance upon the floor,
In chaos, whispers meet the dark,
Reflections echo evermore.

In every crack, a story lives,
Of love, of pain, of dreams we chase,
Through life's wild maze, the heart forgives,
Chaotic beauty, the human grace.

Tides of Thoughtful Distraction

Waves crash on the sandy shore,
Pulling at the mind's own door.
Thoughts drift like leaves on streams,
Caught in the pull of fleeting dreams.

The moon whispers to the night,
Casting shadows, soft and bright.
A dance between focus and drift,
Where clarity and chaos shift.

Eyes wander, hearts take flight,
Chasing wonders, lost in light.
In moments brief, we find our way,
Tides of thought, at play today.

Yet in the stillness, wisdom grows,
In the pauses, deeper flows.
Let distractions weave and twine,
In this tapestry, truth we find.

The Flicker Between Dreams and Reality

In the twilight, shadows dance,
Painted visions, a fleeting chance.
The world blurs in soft shimmer,
As whispers of dreams begin to glimmer.

Reality hums a steady tune,
While dreams dive into the moon.
A flicker caught in a moment's grace,
Where time slows down, and thoughts embrace.

Eyes half-closed, we drift and sway,
Between the night and breaking day.
Each heartbeat echoes a silent plea,
For the magic of what could be.

In this space, we linger long,
Crafting stories, finding song.
Hope and wonder intertwine,
In the flicker of the divine.

Laughter in the Tripping Light

Softly glows the evening sun,
As laughter echoes, hearts have fun.
In the spaces where shadows play,
Joyful moments dance and sway.

Hues of gold on faces bright,
Wandering through the tripping light.
With every giggle, spirits soar,
A melody that begs for more.

Twinkling stars in a twilight glow,
Carry the warmth of tales we know.
Each chuckle rings like summer rain,
In this vivid, sweet refrain.

Embrace the echoes, let them stay,
As laughter lights the evening gray.
For in each chuckle, love ignites,
In the splendor of fleeting nights.

When Delight Interrupts a Train of Thought

A whisper soft, a moment bright,
Delight comes in, igniting light.
Thoughts stumble on a joyous spark,
As laughter trills in the living dark.

Plans laid out, like tracks ahead,
But a smile blooms where reason's tread.
Time pauses, wings unfold,
In the warmth where hearts are bold.

Ideas waltz in whimsical twirl,
As innocent joy starts to unfurl.
In the space where intentions roam,
Delight carves out a cozy home.

So let the echoes, sweet and pure,
Guide your thoughts to landscapes obscure.
For when delight interrupts the train,
Life's journey turns to joyous gain.

Milton Keynes UK
Ingram Content Group UK Ltd.
UKHW021127021124
450571UK00005B/70